Traveling With Toddlers

GAYLE JERVIS
&
KRISTEN JERVIS CACKA

DEDICATION

To our newest blessing, Miss A.

CONTENTS

DISCLAIMER

The authors and the publisher cannot be held responsible for damage, mishap, injury incurred during the use of or because of activities in this book. Appropriate and reasonable caution and adult supervision of children involved in activities and corresponding to the age and capability of each child involved is recommended at all times. Do not leave children unattended at any time. Observe safety and caution at all times. While all attempts have been made to provide effective, verifiable information in this book, neither the author nor publisher assumes responsibility for errors, inaccuracies or omissions.

INTRODUCTION

Traveling with toddlers can either increase your pleasure or convince you to never travel with a toddler again. Whether it is a short trip to a restaurant or to visit friends or a long plane ride, the information and ideas provided here will minimize the frustrations and maximize the joys of traveling with your toddler.

My granddaughter has participated in long road trips and in long plane rides including a flight to Paris. She has climbed the Eiffel Tower with her grandparents and parents, stood in long lines to enter the Louvre and has added to our holiday memories as she entertained us with her curiosity and enthusiasm. On one of my granddaughter's long road trips, I had prepared twenty busy bags that you will be soon reading about. After they were driving about 4 hours, I received an endearing e-mail from my daughter:

> *So the travel bags are a God send. I frantically packed first thing this morning, snagged most of the completed bags and we were set to go. The only thing I made sure V knew is that she had to play with whatever I gave her for 15 min. This has been even easier than I thought it would be. We only turned on music in the last half hour. She loved the play dough and the gluing. Don't include ribbon with glue though since it didn't stick well. I also should have held onto the glue lid since it is now missing :). You are the activity guru!! :)*

From the above e-mail, you have learned that what we are about to tell you has been applied and tested! My daughter has accumulated many practical strategies to lessen the tensions and increase the joy of traveling with her toddler. I have taught professionally and I have home schooled both of my children which has given me the tools to develop activities that will keep toddlers engaged while traveling. Together, we have included all the information you need to have a great trip while traveling with your little one.

In this book, you will discover such information as the following:

- Basic Essentials
- Preparing your Toddler for the Trip
- Packing Your Toddler's Suitcase
- Routines
- Air Travel Tips
- Car Travel Tips
- Travel Busy Bag Activities
- Sight Seeing Activities
- Waiting in Line Activities
- Hotel Room Activities

We hope that as you implement these strategies, you will create wonderful memories as your trip will be enriched when you travel with your toddler.

Gayle Jervis & Kristen Jervis Cacka

CHAPTER 1:

BASIC ESSENTIALS

The following items are a list of essentials that you may need whether you are traveling by car or by plane. As you look through this list, you may feel overwhelmed by the number of items. Certainly, traveling with a toddler does take up more space in your car and may require you to pay for extra luggage when you are flying. However, many items such as a playpen may not be necessary if you are traveling by hotel where you can request a crib. Other items such as a booster seat may not be necessary if someone can provide them when you reach your destination. However, we have included as many items as possible to alleviate your anxiety that you are forgetting something when you make your own list. All you have to do is go through each of the items and customize your own list of essentials.

PASSPORT AND CONSENT LETTERS

If you are flying to another country, you will need a passport for your toddler. The International Civil Aviation Organization recommends a "one passport, one person" policy that requires every individual regardless of age who travels by air to have his or her own document. Please check your country's policy to apply for your child's passport.

Information for Passports for Children from Passport Canada:
http://www.ppt.gc.ca/info/16-.aspx

Passport United States:
http://travel.state.gov/passport/get/minors/minors_834.html

If you are traveling alone with your child, you will need to carry a consent letter from your child's other guardian. It is not a legal requirement in Canada, but immigration authorities may still request one when you enter or leave a foreign country. However, every country has its own entry and exit requirements and carrying a consent letter does not guarantee that your child will be allowed in the country or allowed to leave. Check the following link from the Government of Canada for instructions on how to write a consent letter: http://travel.gc.ca/travelling/children/conse nt-letter.

It is strongly recommended that the consent letter to travel be notarized by a notary public so that the validity of the letter will not be questioned.

ON THE GO BAG

This bag is required whether you are traveling by car or plane. Your diaper bag may be appropriate to carry the following items but you may need something larger. I have used a large diaper bag for airplane trips and tote bags and file boxes for car trips.

Essentials For Your Bag:

- Change of clothes for your toddler

- Change of shirt for you to feel a little more "put together" if you will be immediately arriving at someone's place

- Diapers for 1 to 2 days. The extra is for any unexpected situations such as your plane is stuck on the runway

- Changing pad

- Snacks

- Busy bags and other activities

- Medical Kit. See more information below.

- iPad, Kindle, Headphones, etc

- Small purse or wallet

MEDICAL KIT

Keep a first aid kit in your car for traveling and take one with you when you are going on an airplane. Choose small travel size items and keep in a small container such as a cosmetic bag. Include such items as the following:

- Bandages

- Antibacterial wipes

- Package of tissues

- Children's Tylenol

- Antibacterial cream

- Cleansing wipes

- Nail file

- Chewable Children's Dramamine or Gravol for motion sickness

- Children's ear plugs to relieve ear and sinus pain

- Saline Drops to lessen the effects of air pressure on your toddler's ears

- Hand Sanitizer

- Insect spray (If flying, keep in suitcase)

- Sun screen lotion (If flying, keep in suitcase)

SUITCASE

There are many suitcases available for children that are decorated in their favorite movie or television show. While personalized luggage is also available, we do not recommend it for your child's protection. Also, most of these novelty suitcases share one major disadvantage: the pull along mechanism is made for the height of a toddler. Since it will be you who will end up pulling the suitcase when your toddler tires of the novelty of being in control of his own suitcase, make sure the handle is long enough for your comfort.

You may also opt not to buy a child's suitcase and use a duffel bag that you already own. That may be a good choice as long as the bag has wheels and a strap to pull.

We really like the Trunki Suitcase for air travel. The Trunki Suitcase is popular for the following reasons:

- It is made of very durable hard plastic.

- It can be checked in at the airport as hand luggage.

- Your toddler can use it as a ride on toy and it can be pulled. This is a great feature when your child is tired or when you need to stand in a long line.

- The strap to pull the suitcase is long enough for an adult to pull, and can also be used to carry as an over the shoulder bag.

Website: http://www.trunki.com/trunki

BACKPACK

A backpack is particularly useful when you are sightseeing. You can store in it your camera, a bottle of water, snacks, jackets, and a small bag that has a changing pad, plastic bag, and diaper. If you have someone to help you, you will also want to include your child's carrier in your backpack so that when he tires of walking, you can carry him on your back. See more information below about children's carriers.

The most obvious drawback to a backpack is that if it isn't carefully chosen, it can quickly become cumbersome as the straps begin to dig into your shoulders.

Consider the following tips when you look for a backpack:

- The weight of a backpack should rest primarily on your hips. Your back, shoulders and upper pectoral region carry the rest of the weight secondarily.

- One of the most important criterion for a backpack is that it must fit your torso.

- Go to a store that will put some weight in the backpack to help you determine how a typical pack load will feel.

- Look for a backpack that has ventilation since it can get really warm carrying it on your back all day.

Certainly the usefulness of a backpack depends on whether you have someone else with you as you travel with your toddler. Inevitably, your toddler will want to be carried at some point! Assess the nature of your holiday to decide whether you will only need a stroller and a small bag in its storage. Because we found that strollers were often a nuisance in the crowded streets of Paris, the backpack and child carrier were continually used.

FABRIC HIGH CHAIR

This item has been included under our list of basic essentials even though it won't be necessary unless you are traveling in Europe.

Fortunately, my sister-in-law and brother had been to France with their two sons before we went and they informed us that many restaurants were not child friendly as they didn't offer high chairs or booster seats. Therefore, we bought a fabric high chair which was indispensable as we toured Paris! We used the My Little Seat Infant Travel High Chair.

BOOSTER SEAT

If you are stopping at someone's place during a road trip, come prepared with a booster seat. Stacking books on a chair and covering them with a towel is an option but having a booster seat helps to prevent unruly behavior. We like the Fisher-Price Healthy Care Booster Seat since it can be adjusted height wise as your toddler grows and it folds compactly for easy traveling.

We recognize that taking this booster seat is too cumbersome if you are traveling by plane. Therefore, if you are visiting someone at your destination, see if they can borrow a high chair or booster seat from a friend. When I was staying in Palm Springs for several weeks, we were able to find one at a consignment store.

STROLLER

If you are going on a trip that involves lots of walks with smooth sidewalks and paths, you will need your stroller.

If you don't already have one, here are a few tips to consider when you choose a stroller for traveling:

- Be able to tilt the stroller back to make it easier for your toddler to fall asleep

- Buy a rain cover and sun cover for your stroller if you expect lots of rain or lots of sunshine.

- Buy a snack tray such as the Star Kids Snack & Play Travel Tray to accommodate snacks and small toys and books to read.

- Add a stroller hook to your stroller to hang any extra bags. However, please be careful not to exceed the weight of your child and stroller with bags or your stroller could tip when you take your child out!

- Choose a stroller that folds easily and compactly. This feature is incredibly important when you must quickly fold it up to get on a bus or train.

- Find a stroller that has a footrest to add to your toddler's comfort.

- Some strollers are built more for babies so make sure the seat is wide enough and the backrest is high enough for your toddler's comfort.

- Make sure the handle height is high enough for your comfort to push the stroller. Many strollers are designed for a person about 5'6" which on a longer trip can be frustrating for taller parents.

PLAYPEN

Consider the following factors to determine whether you need to take a playpen with you:

1. When you reach your destination, is a playpen available? If you are staying at a resort or hotel, will they provide you with a crib or playpen?

2. If you are renting a vacation home, is it cost efficient to rent a playpen or crib or bring your own?

3. If you think your child will be most settled and comfortable sleeping in something familiar, you may opt to take your own playpen.

HARNESS

When we went to France, I purchased a child's harness. I wanted our daughter to have the independence to walk freely without me worrying about her safety. An added benefit was walking without tiring her little arm from having to hold our hands for any length of time. We used the Little Life Harness as it was quite slim and easy to pack in our backpack. This harness eliminated our anxieties and eliminated any imminent tantrums because she enjoyed her independence.

Check our website (busytoddlerhappymom.com) to see how we used this harness when we went hiking.

CHILD CARRIER

You may think that as long as you have a stroller or harness, you don't need a child carrier. However, if your trip includes a lot of sightseeing or hiking, this carrier can be indispensable. If you are in a crowd of people, you will most likely become stressed as you push your little person in her stroller or as you allow her to walk. She may also become agitated since all she can see are feet and if she looks a little higher, only people's stomachs. If she is being pushed in a stroller, the ride may be a little uncomfortable if she is being pushed on cobbled sidewalks like those in France. We also found that there were many places that asked visitors to leave their strollers outside the buildings. Inside the Louvre, while my daughter, Miss V, was fresh, she walked with her harness. However, as she tired and as it became more crowded, we switched to carrying her in the child carrier. When it was time for a nap, my husband or myself just put the top of the carrier over her head and from the vibrations of the walk, she quietly fell asleep. We used the Ergo Baby Carrier.

It is important to buy a carrier that has the following features:

- The majority of the weight must be carried on your hips. The straps should not be digging into your shoulders. Therefore, fit the pack from your hips up rather than your shoulders down.

- Look for a carrier that is not very bulky, so that it fits easily in your luggage or backpack.

- If you're going somewhere hot, choose one that is made of moisture-resistant fabric or breathable material.

- Choose a carrier that allows you to carry your child either on your back or on your hip. This feature is good for the adult to have a break from one position and it is good for the toddler who also wants a new position for viewing.

TRAY FOR STROLLER AND CAR SEAT

If you have a tray for your stroller and car seat, you now have so many more possibilities to keep your child occupied. You are giving your toddler some independence as he plays with toys or eats snacks that you have placed on the tray. We have really liked the Star Kids

Snack & Play Travel Tray, since it has tall sides. Also it has a wide surface, great for reading books and for playing with busy bags.

CHILDREN'S HEADPHONES

You may not need headphones on a road trip, but they are definitely useful on flights. Remember that it is important to buy headphones that will not damage your child's hearing. Many auditory health organizations caution parents that the noise level should be no higher than 85 decibels for young children. This concern is resolved by buying children's headphones that limit the volume.

SMART PHONE/DVD PLAYER/TABLET

Your toddler may already be technically savvy, asking to play with your smart phone. We have occupied my daughter's time on many a shopping trip by letting her look at photos on my phone!

Here are some suggestions on how to use technology to occupy your child's time:

- Many people own an iPad or Tablet and can download several movies for their toddler on it. However, you may want to consider buying a DVD Compact player. Setting it up on your flight table makes it easier for your child to see the movie and prevents your child from wanting to sit on the edge of her seat trying to see the small images on the plane's screen. Both the iPad and DVD serve the same purpose except that there is less to touch using the DVD player. Using either one is often a good idea since not all flights have a movie and the movie may not be appropriate for your toddler.

- Download e-book picture books since it is too cumbersome to take as many books as your child may like to read.

- Record stories from books he loves so that he can listen to your voice as he turns the pages.

- Check out some Toddler Apps.

- Download some favorite children's songs for your toddler to listen to. Download some upbeat songs for his enjoyment, but also, download some slower music to help him fall asleep."

CAR SEAT

If you are flying and then need a car when you reach your destination, you may want to contact the car rental to see how much they charge to rent a car seat rather than lugging yours with you. Otherwise, we recommend purchasing a car seat bag to protect your car seat when it is in checked luggage. Most airlines do provide bags for the car seat but from time to time they do run out and then your expensive car seat is left unprotected.

GRO-CLOCK

Gro-Clocks are helpful in maintaining routines regardless of time zone or destination. My daughter is used to the routine of someone coming for her when the Sun on the clock comes up, either in the morning or after Quiet Time. Therefore, she is much more content to wait or play in her playpen or bed. If there are stars still showing on the clock, your toddler learns that it isn't time to get up yet. When the sun shows up on the screen, it is time to call for Mommy or Daddy! If you are unfamiliar with the Gro Clock, it has stars in the sky around a moon on the face of the clock when it is still sleep time.

BOOKS

For your child's independent use, take only board books or cheap picture books. Don't take favorite books that you don't want mutilated or even lost. In fact, consider going to a consignment store and stocking up on some cheap books for your trip.

If you are traveling by plane, you will be more restricted by the number of books you can take. However, if you have a Tablet or iPad, you could download some children's books. When you reach your destination, look for a thrift store to stock up on more books.

CHAPTER 2:

PREPARING YOUR TODDLER FOR A TRIP

Since I was a child, my parents have enjoyed relating the story of how when I was 2.5 years old, my personality changed while my family and I were on holiday. At each hotel, I continually asked sadly, "Is this home?". By the time we were driving to yet another city, I became quite aggressive and began hitting my older brother. We had a very amicable relationship and so my brother, rather startled by this behavior, merely held his head to protect himself. My parents learned the hard way how important it is to prepare your child for a trip! Apparently I changed from being "adorable" to "fearsome" - most likely because my parents hadn't prepared me well enough for all the new experiences I would have while on holiday.

The following are some suggestions to help your toddler adapt well to all the new situations that will occur when she travels:

- Your toddler may be going to various types of restaurants on this trip. To gain confidence that your toddler can do this and to give him practice of what is expected from him, go to a couple of local restaurants with him before you leave. Eating at a more formal restaurant is possible with a toddler if you dine when she is hungry and not so late that she is exhausted.

- When you visit museums or art galleries, you will quickly notice how quiet the room is even if it is filled with people. There are some places that are not as child-friendly as others. Therefore, it is imperative that your toddler learns before you leave what you mean by using your "soft voice".

- The following are activities to practice being quiet:

  o Make a game of using your loud voice and then your soft voice.

  o Give him a wooden spoon and let him tap loudly on the floor and then softly.

o Give him a baby doll and tell him to speak softly to the baby.

o Pretend you are at a basketball game and cheer loudly and then pretend you are in a museum and whisper softly.

o Using your toddler's play food, pretend you are eating at a restaurant. Talk softly, then talk loudly. When you talk loudly, practice having to leave the restaurant. Practice talking softly and tell your toddler how pleased everyone is that we are talking quietly.

o Look for opportunities to praise your toddler for speaking softly such as when he is shopping with you.

o Listen to your voice to make sure you aren't speaking loudly to him as you tell him to speak softly!

• Talk about what your toddler needs to pack in his suitcase. Have a trial run several times as you get your toddler's help packing his suitcase. What clothes will he need? What toys will he take? Put some things in the suitcase that aren't appropriate such as an out of season jacket and have him pull it out. Get him excited about leaving home for a little while. Explain to him that he is going on an adventure.

- If you are expecting your child to sleep in a playpen rather than a crib, make sure he has been sleeping in the playpen at least during his naps so that this practice isn't foisted on him abruptly when he is traveling.

- Teach your toddler some fun traveling songs. Download a collection of children's music that she will be able to listen to on the plane or in the car using her headphones. However, if you are driving, it would even be more enjoyable for all of you to listen and to sing these songs. Teach her such songs as: Old MacDonald Had a Farm, If You're Happy And You Know It, and You Are My Sunshine.

- Show your toddler photos from holidays you have already had as you talk about the one you will soon be taking.

- Show photos of places and people you expect to see. The internet should have pictures of your sight seeing destinations. Make sure you talk about how much fun it is to see new places and to see people you don't get to see very often.

- Do some pretend play as you show him what will happen at the airport when he must go through security. Take your shoes off and put any other items in a container and pretend it is going though a special machine. I once forgot to take off my belt when carrying Miss V through security and when the buzzer went off, both of us were searched. Thankfully, Miss V thought it was a fun game to raise her arms and be searched rather than having a fearful meltdown when a stranger touched her.

The following is a list of picture books to help you talk about your trip. After you read a book, talk about the trip you are planning. Explain how you are going on a long car ride or perhaps you are flying in an airplane. Talk about what you are going to see and do.

- *Toot & Puddle* by Holly Hobbie: Toot decides to travel and see the world, but Puddle chooses to stay at home. Puddle then decides to have some adventures at home while he waits for Toot's return.

- *It's Vacation Time: Playtime with Little Nye* by Lerryn Korda: Little Nye is packing far too many things in his suitcase and Lester offers to lighten the load by taking out items.

- *Maisy Goes On Vacation* by Lucy Cousins: While Maisy goes on a train heading to the seashore, she enjoys coloring and eating snacks. When she arrives, she collects seashells, and builds sandcastles at the beach.

- *Maisy Goes to The Museum* by Lucy Cousins: Maisy and her friends tour a museum exploring everything from dinosaurs to a moon exhibit.

- *A Vacation For Pooch* by Maryann Cocca-Leffler: Violet and Pooch pack to go on their two different vacations. However, they get their bags mixed up when they arrive at their destinations.

- *Bears' Vacation* by Stan and Jan Berenstain: Before Little Bear can enjoy the beach, Papa Bear wants to teach him some safety rules. A humorous story as Papa Bear often gets into trouble by not practicing these safety rules.

- *Airplanes: Soaring! Diving! Turning* by Patricia Hubbell: The author describes in rhyming text different kinds of airplanes such as cargo planes, jumbo jets, propeller planes, hydroplanes etc.

- *Fred and Ted Like to Fly* by Peter Eastman: Fred and Ted fly to a tropical island to enjoy the beach.

- *Fred and Ted's Road Trip* by Peter Eastman: Fred and Ted go on a road trip and encounter things that don't go according to plan such as muddy roads, a storm, and flat tires.

- *Are We There Yet?* by Sam Williams: Mama takes her four bored ducklings on a journey

- *Arthur's Family Vacation* by Marc Brown: Arthur goes on a road trip with his family.

Below are some picture books and activities that we included in our first book, Busy Toddler, Happy Mom. Use these books and activities to discuss more about the trip you are planning and to increase her excitement and enthusiasm.

- *My Car* by Byron Barton

    o Fill a dishpan with soap and water and have your toddler wash her toy cars. Create a road with masking tape and suggest he drives the car to get some oil for the car, to go shopping, and to look for a place to park. Remind him to "honk his horn" when some people start crossing the road. In other words, you are showing him how to repeat what occurred in the book.

- *Sea, Sand and Me* by Patricia Hubbell

    o Create your own beach by putting a blanket on the floor and pretend it is the beach. Lay your beach towels on top of this blanket. Pack a tote bag with beach items such as sun hat, sandals, beach ball, pail and shovel and bathing suit. Let her enjoy taking out these items to play with. Play with the beach ball by rolling it back and forth to each other. Make sure you and your toddler prepare a snack or lunch to take to the beach. Before you read this book, make a big batch of play dough so that you can make play dough castles. Add some seashells and twigs to the "sand castle."

- *Cars* by Patricia Hubbell

    o Give your toddler a tour of your car as you point out the following: steering wheel, hubcaps, wheels, headlights, windshield wipers, turning signal, and gas tank. You could even open up the hood and show her inside the engine.

    o After the tour of your car, set up a long board or large cardboard on an incline for your child to drive his cars.

- *Airport* by Byron Barton

  o Have your child pretend he is an airplane by holding his arms out and traveling through the room "flying."

  o Set up some chairs so that you have an aisle in the middle. Tell your toddler that she is the pilot who is going to fly this airplane. Have her get her dolls and plush animals to be the passengers. For extra fun, give your toddler a white shirt and dark tie to wear when she is a pilot. Give her the lid of a large ice cream pail to use as her steering wheel. When she sits in the pilot's seat, ask her if the plane is ready for takeoff. Tell her that you are the flight attendant who takes care of the passengers. While she flies the plane, you can role-play how a flight attendant tells everyone to wear a seat belt. As flight attendant, you can serve people "food and drinks. Then switch roles so that your toddler can be a flight attendant. Perhaps replace the tie with a scarf for a change in costume. This time you can pretend that you are a passenger receiving her care.

CHAPTER 3:

PACKING YOUR TODDLER'S SUITCASE

When you begin packing your toddler's suitcase, here are some ideas you may find helpful:

- Check the airline you are flying to see which items to pack in your carry-on and which items must go in your checked baggage. The following link from Canadian Air Transport Security Authority gives a detailed list of what is carry on and what must be checked: http://www.catsa.gc.ca/complete-item-list

- Make a comprehensive packing list. Here are some things to consider:

- Who is in your traveling party?

- Where are you flying to?

- How many bags are you bringing?

- Are your toddler's clothes going in a carry on, in your suitcase or in their own suitcase?

- What is the expected weather?

- What are your accommodation?

- What type of holiday are you planning? Sightseeing? Visiting? Beach Vacation?

- How long is your trip?

- Plan your toddler's outfits based on the types of activities he will be doing. For example, what he will need to wear when he sees a favorite aunt, visits the museum, goes to the zoo, and goes out to a restaurant etc.

- Below is a list of items to help you start your own customized list:

  o Pajamas

  o Socks/Leggings

  o Diapers/Underwear

  o Shirts

  o Shorts

  o Skirts/Tunics

  o Sandals

o Running Shoes

o Sweater

o Jacket

o Sun Hat

o Swimsuit

o Toothbrush

o Toothpaste

o Brush/Comb

o Hair accessories

o Favorite Blanket

o Sunglasses

- Don't pack the day before you leave. Begin collecting your items and set them out in one place. This gives you time to assess whether you really need certain items and gives you time to add what you have forgotten.

- Keep the number of suitcases to a minimum. Therefore, is it possible for you and your spouse to share a suitcase or for you and your toddler to share a suitcase?

- Whether you are going for one week or three weeks, pack the same quantity of clothing. Whether you are staying at a hotel or at someone's place, you can always find a place to wash your clothes to start your second week of holidays.

- Consider the following two packing methods:

  1. Pack together COMPLETE outfits. Some people like to pack each outfit in individual plastic bags. Include a diaper, your child's outfit and his socks. As it is sometimes difficult to anticipate what you are going to need each day, you may need to dress your toddler in layers to prepare for a cool morning and a warm day.

  2. Pack LIKE items together: shirts in one packing container, pants and shorts in another container, etc.

- Consider what packing organizers will be helpful. We tend to use a variety of the following packing organizers:

  1. **Compression Bag:** If you must bring something bulky like a coat, consider using a compression bag.

You merely place the coat in this triple-laminated plastic bag, and roll the air out through its one-way valve. This will flatten the bag and create up to 80% more packing space.

However, this method does wrinkle clothes so that the clothing needs to be wrinkle-free.

2. **Pack It Folders:** Consider using packing folders if you need to take dressy shirts and dresses. There is a special folding board to help you fold each article and each item stacks neatly inside the mesh. They provide great wrinkle resistance while keeping all the clothing compressed and organized. Make sure you add a label on the pack- it folders for quick retrieval. However, the smallest size is 15" so make sure it fits your child's suitcase. One brand we like is Eagle Creek.

3. **Packing Cubes:** We also like packing cubes that come in different sizes and some are two-sided. The two sided works really

well for your toddler's clothes as you can pack his tops on one side and his bottoms on the other side. The one-sided cube works well for such toiletries as shampoo, body wash, and face cloth. Make sure you put labels on the cubes for easy retrieval.

- Think about the order you want to pack items. For instance, pack your toddler's shoes in a bag and place at the bottom of the suitcase. Pack your toddler's pajamas at the top for quick and easy access.

- Tie a brightly colored ribbon or scrap of fabric on your toddler's suitcase so that it can be easily seen if you are looking for it on the baggage carousel.

- Inside the suitcase, tape on the inside lid the contact information of your destination or of your home phone number.

- If your child is still in diapers, pack enough for the first couple days and then plan to buy more there. If you are flying and your child has only been recently trained, consider giving him some pull-ups to wear on the plane since accidents can happen.

- Include a large reusable bag for dirty clothes. If you use cloth diapers, you may already have an appropriate waterproof laundry bag.

- Include in your suitcase extra plastic bags. They can be used to plug a tub or sink drain or store wet and dirty clothes or bathing suits. To take up even less space, buy some doggie bags that are in rolls and are available at the Dollar Store.

- Keep extras toys to a minimum. Since you will be taking an assortment of busy bags and storing them in your toddler's tote bag, you won't need very many toys.

- Some people like to have one communal bag if they are making overnight stops at hotels. They have one change of clothes for everyone, pajamas and toiletries. This simplifies having to open up everyone's suitcases in one cramped room.

- Most of the ideas we have listed for packing your child's suitcase can also be applied to packing your own. However, there are many websites that will give you even more ideas that apply to adults such as how to pack jewelry and your toiletries. http://www.womansday.com/life/tra vel-tips/smart-carry-on-luggage-packing-tips-101797

CHAPTER 4:
ROUTINES

Establishing routines for children are important since their predictability gives them stability and a sense of control. For toddlers especially, routines are important since they have little or no control of their surroundings. Routines help these little people create some sense of their day since they know what to expect. When your toddler goes on a holiday, often their routines disappear and we wonder why they become more demanding and even succumb to temper tantrums. Obviously, maintaining all the routines you have established at home are not possible when you are traveling. However, do your best to maintain some of them to reduce your toddler's anxiety and apprehension.

Think about what routines you can continue:

- What morning routines can be practiced? Is there a particular time he gets up in the morning? Any favorite breakfasts?

- What time is he used to eating lunch? Again, what are his favorite meals? It is so easy to forget what time it is when you are sightseeing and not eat during the times you do when at home. Therefore, try to be much more aware of those necessary morning and afternoon snacks and of course, do your best to eat lunch and supper when your toddler is used to having those meals.

- Do you put on her pajamas when she has a nap? Does she like to sleep with a particular blanket or plush animal? Do you read a book to her?

- Does he sleep best when there are no distractions? If you are flying, attach a scarf around the table in front of you and create a tent so that he can fall asleep. If you are driving, pull down the solar shade beside her window.

- Does your toddler nap at a certain time each day? Does he sleep with a favorite stuffed animal?

- Does she go to bed at the same time each night?

- Is your toddler freshest in the morning? or afternoon?

- Perhaps the wisest routine to put in place during your holiday is to quit before all of you are exhausted. So often, we create a travel itinerary that is unrealistic and unless we are adaptable and realize that seeing less may be seeing more, you could set yourselves up for an anxious holiday.

CHAPTER 5:

HOW TO HANDLE TANTRUMS & MISBEHAVIOR

Below are some basic things to consider if your toddler is acting up while you are traveling. While I don't believe parents are responsible for all our children's misbehaviors, we must at least ask is there any way I have contributed to my child's change in behavior if it occurs during your trip.

1. Have you prepared your child well enough for a holiday?

Sometimes the tears are a result of too much strangeness. Their level of understanding is just not that advanced and some children especially react to being pulled away from everything that is familiar.

Other children decide that there is only one person they want to be with which puts terrible pressure on that adult. My daughter decided that her dad was the only person who could carry her when we first began sightseeing in Paris. Sometimes you feel trapped since you don't want your child to become even louder and more obnoxious when you try to transfer him to another adult. Therefore, you let this demand continue until the adult has carried him to exhaustion and the other adults are unable to help. In our case, we decided to take a stand and to allow Grandma and Grandpa to play a more important support role. The first day was a little rough but it was worth it since during the rest of the trip she went to all of the adults.

2. **Attempt to distract your toddler from her misbehavior.**

Have you been providing enough stimulation and activities to keep your toddler entertained? Have you been giving her enough one on one attention?

3. **Did you remember to give your child some things that are familiar to help compensate for all the strangeness she**

is witnessing?

4. Remember to relax when your child cries even if the walls are thin.

One thing a child easily absorbs is your anxiety and your emotions can feed on each other!

5. Do you have unrealistic expectations concerning your toddler's behavior?

For instance, unless your child has been toilet trained for some time, it is much easier if your child wears a disposable diaper. Often, a bathroom isn't accessible quickly enough when your child decides he needs one!

We also may be expecting our toddler to be stationary and quiet beyond his ability. If you are traveling with another family who has a toddler there can be comparisons which are really unfair since each child's temperaments are different and one child can sit longer and sit more quietly than another child.

If you are unaccustomed to traveling with a

child, you may look longingly at a restaurant that looks really quaint and relaxing. However, it may not necessarily be suitable for your toddler. Generally, whenever we can find a restaurant where we can sit outside, or be in a relaxing, child friendly venue, we choose that. Also, whenever we find a deli, we plan a picnic in a park. Therefore, it is only for special occasions that we add a little more pressure on our toddler to behave especially well in places that aren't child friendly.

6. **Is your child reacting since you are not making time for naps and early bedtimes?**

Probably the most important point to avoid behavior problems is to ask yourself if your toddler is getting enough sleep. Will Wilkoff in his book, <u>How to Say No To Your Toddler</u> writes, "Sleep deprivation can turn your usually compliant two-year-old into a demon and it will weaken your resolve to follow through with consequences. ... Like you, your toddler's patience decreases and her frustration level increases when she gets tired." (72, 75)

This same author lists some warning signs that your child is overtired:

- She sleeps fewer than twelve hours in a twenty-four-hour day
- You must wake her in the morning
- She wants her blanket or security object frequently
- She sucks her thumb frequently. She falls asleep after just a few minutes of a car ride.
- She wakes frequently at night with what appears to be nightmares. (76)

7. **Is your toddler's temperament affected by the type of food she is eating?**

Pay attention to how often she is receiving a meal or snack that has little nutritional value.

Many of us don't eat as healthy when we are traveling. That occurs because it isn't always as easy or as quick to find wholesome foods, but it may also be that we give ourselves permission to buy that extra burger and fries and to buy that chocolate coated donut. The problem is that we may also be giving our toddler more greasy and sugary foods than what he is used to eating at home. This change in diet could also change his temperament.

ADDITIONAL RESOURCES

How to Say No To Your Toddler by Will Wilkoff

Setting Limits with your Strong-Willed Child by Robert MacKenzie - The author gives tips on how to establish your relationship with your child based on mutual respect and cooperation rather than conflict.

Toddler Tantrum Advice and Tricks: http://www.parenting.com/article/toddler-tantrum-advice?page=0,1"

CHAPTER 6:
SNACKS

Snacks can entertain your toddler while keeping him happy between meals. Choosing appropriate snacks can even give a boost to your toddler's nutritional levels. Therefore, having snacks ready for your toddler during your holiday is very important.

As you make your list of what snacks to bring, consider the following:

1. Give your child snacks that you know he already likes. Toddlers are happiest with the familiar and this is yet another way to provide him with what he is accustomed to. If you want to introduce a new snack, make sure you give it to him before you leave to see if he likes it.

2. Snacks require your close supervision

since a toddler may still stuff too much food in his mouth and begin gagging. Therefore, exercise caution where you give him these snacks. If you are planning on eating in the car, make sure that he can eat that particular snack safely without your intervention. Remember that you don't have as quick access to your toddler when you also are strapped in your seat with a seat belt.

3. Try to make "nutrient-dense" snacks a priority. Avoid prepackaged, processed snacks which are high in sugar, salt and fat. Too much sugar may give your toddler a stomach ache or even increase his aggressive behavior.

4. Consider which snacks are less messy and require less intervention from you. Some snacks require your help if they need a spoon so obviously that won't be a good option while he is sitting in the back seat of the car.

5. Carry some cleansing wipes for quick cleaning of hands and face.

6. The following are suggested snacks that work well for traveling in the car and in the plane.

- Unsalted pretzels
- String cheese
- Small boxes of raisins
- Granola Bars
- Fresh fruit
- Applesauce and other fruit cups
- Individual containers of yogurt
- Muffins
- Crackers
- Cut up vegetables and dip
- Whole Grain Cereal
- Banana Chips
- Roasted Chickpeas
- Goldfish Crackers

7. Snacks can be put in small plastic baggies or small snack containers.

CHAPTER 7:

PACKING THE CAR

Consider the following ideas as you prepare for a road trip.

1. Here are a few things you need to check so that you are confident of your car's reliability, safety and comfort:

   • Consider the possible driving conditions that are associated with snow, rain, heat or freezing temperatures.

   • Do the tires have enough air?

   • Have you had the oil changed?

   • Are there any illuminated warning lights that you have been ignoring?

   • Have you cleaned out the interior and the trunk to get rid of everything you do not need for this trip?

- Do you have a container filled with items that may help you during any unexpected emergencies such as the following: flares, jumper cables, a small case of tools, a flashlight, batteries, a pocket knife and a wind-up radio.

2. Before you leave on your trip, prepare some of the busy bags and other activities we have listed for you later in this book.

3. Make a list of everything you want to put in the car besides suitcases. Are you taking a cooler for snacks and lunches? Are you taking beach chairs? Bikes? Skis?

   - After you have made your list, you may discover you are bringing more than what you can realistically pack in your car. Can you eliminate some items or do you need a roof carrier?

4. Consider taking a cooler or an insulated bag. Keep inside it bottles of water, a cutting board, a cutting knife, plastic utensils, disposable plates and bowls, napkins, cleaning wipes, can opener, and plastic tablecloth. When you start your trip, fill it with snacks and a possible lunch. After using up your initial supplies, pick up

some deli meat, cheese and buns for your daily lunches. Your toddler will enjoy these picnics since he won't have as many restraints as he would in a restaurant and will probably get some exercise running around outside.

5. Do you have a Medical Kit packed? Check our list of Basic Essentials to know what to include.

6. Pack your car based on when you will need particular items. In other words, if your cooler is in the trunk, keep it accessible and not hiding behind all your luggage.

7. Pack the car the night before since it always takes longer than you think to get it ready for departure.

8. Have a trash bin for the front seat and back seat. It can be as simple as a large cereal container that has a flip back lid. Place a plastic bag inside it to empty quickly. Also, it can be used as a vomit bag if you discover your child has motion sickness!

9. For extra convenience, place a diaper, individual baby wipes, plastic bag and changing pad in the glove compartment for fast retrieval.

10. Double check your packing to ensure that everything is secured safely so that nothing can go flying and hit someone in the car if you have to brake suddenly. Do not pack anything higher than the level of the rear seats so that the driver's view is not obscured.

11. Consider adding a backseat organizer that you hook to the back of the front passenger seat.

12. If you don't already have a sunshade attached to your toddler's side window, consider buying one for your road trip to block the sun's rays.

13. Pack your On The Go bag or file box of the various items suggested in Basic Essentials. Storing it on the floor by your feet in the front seat is ideal for easy access. However, you may need to keep it on the floor in the back seat, but then you will need to anticipate what snacks and busy bags you are going to use until your next rest stop and keep them with you in the front seat.

14. Place a partial roll of paper towels on the side door's storage compartment for ready access if you have any spills.

15. If your child is potty-trained, take a portable potty rather than hope that she can wait until you find an appropriate rest area.

16. Consider what time you will start your trip. Here are some possibilities:

    a. Leave shortly before you're child's bedtime or nap time. Put on her pajamas, read her a book, give her favorite animal she sleeps with and put her in her car seat. The disadvantage to this strategy is that the driver may also be tired and it could be unsafe for him to drive too long into the evening.

    b. Leave just before a meal so that your toddler is already preoccupied for awhile as he eats while you drive.

    c. Leave before your child typically wakes up such as 4am. This allows you to get some sleep but to still transfer a sleeping child to the car so you can drive several hours without needing to entertain.

17. Remember to have some children's music ready to play during your trip.

18. Check out playgrounds and rest stops on Google Maps. It is a great way to find nice

rest stops and see if there are bathrooms at this particular site. Please note that this works best for heavily populated areas.

EXTRA RESOURCES

The following link is a great site to look at while you prepare your car for this trip since it includes items for each of the following categories: car essentials, car comforts, emergency kit, first aid kit, and cold weather driving.

http://www.planningroadtrips.com/packing/car/

CHAPTER 8:

AIR TRAVEL TIPS

There is nothing worse than planning your trip through the airport expecting to use your stroller only to discover that it is too large and must be checked. Or your flight has been delayed getting off the ground and you are already running out of diapers. These and other challenges can be prevented if you are well prepared for your flight. This section on air travel will give you the information you need about what to know before you get on the plane, what to know while on the plane, and how to manage jet lag.

WHAT TO KNOW BEFORE YOU GET ON THE PLANE

1. A child two years of age and older must have his own seat. However, if you can

afford paying for that extra seat even when your child is a younger toddler, What to Know While on the Plane, that extra space will be really helpful. Or, when you are checking in, ask if there are any vacant seats so that you could have more room.

2. Check with your airline to see what extra luggage and carry-ons you may bring with you for your child.

3. Check your airlines for its specifications if you take a stroller. Generally, a stroller with a collapsed diameter not exceeding 25.5. centimetres (10 inches) and a length not exceeding 92 centimetres (36 inches) is allowed plus your own carry-on allowance. It can be checked at the gate to be delivered to you at the aircraft door at the end of your flight. Make sure your stroller is labeled for easy access as a Gate Check item. However, if you travel with a large, heavy stroller, you may need to check it in and it will count as one piece of baggage toward the maximum number of checked bags allowed by your fare type.

4. If your flight includes a meal, make sure you request a child's meal. Even then, bring extra food for your child since he may be served something he doesn't like or he may want an additional snack during the flight.

5. Check your airlines so that you know how to choose your seat, how early you need to check in, and whether it offers free movies. When you request seats, try to get an outside aisle so that you can take your toddler for regular walks without bothering another passenger. Also, check with the airline to know what size of water and juice containers you can bring for your toddler.

6. Think ahead to simplify going through security. For instance, wear slip on shoes and have the items you need to take out of your bag, such as liquids, stored in a small plastic bag for quick removal.

7. Keep in your tote bag a diaper, changing pad, a change of clothes, some baby wipes, and a plastic bag for the disposal of the diaper. Carry a diaper for every hour of the flight even

though it is usually more than is needed but comes in very handy if your flight is delayed!

8. Choose easy care comfortable clothes to wear on the plane for both you and your toddler. Dress your child in a couple of light layers, so you can add or remove layers as necessary.

9. Make sure you have water before getting on the plane. Either purchase a bottle of water or bring a water bottle to fill after security. Often, the flight attendants cannot give you a drink when the seatbelt light is on or if there is any turbulence. Be prepared for such scenarios and have snacks and drinks ready for your toddler.

WHAT TO KNOW WHILE ON THE PLANE

1. When you get to your seats on the plane, use some of your antibacterial wipes and clean the seats and table surfaces. This one action may help prevent any sickness that often occurs after a lengthy plane trip.

2. Put your bag that includes activities and snacks under the seat in front of you for easy access.

3. Even if your toddler is potty trained, consider giving her pull-ups to wear since a little bit of anxiety combined with the vibrations of the plane are conducive to your toddler having accidents. Also, just when your toddler wants the toilet, there may be a line up and he is unable to wait. If you don't want to do that, have extra clothes and perhaps a small towel to access quickly if she does have an accident.

4. Take your toddler for regular walks on the plane as long as the seatbelt sign is off.

5. Make sure you know where the vomit bag is in the pocket of the seat in front of you, just in case you have turbulent weather and your flight is not very smooth. If you know your child gets motion sick in a car, you might want to consider giving her children's Gravol. Be sure to check the appropriate dosage.

6. Some children are sensitive to the change in air pressure when they are

flying. This change in cabin pressure mainly occurs during takeoff and during descent. During those times, try some of the following suggestions to help prevent ear pain:

- Give her lots to drink throughout the flight.

- Make a game of yawning.

- Give her some snacks which not only increases her swallowing but provides a distraction from her discomfort.

- Use children's ear plugs to help decrease the pressure. She may resist wearing them unless you turn it into a game and you wear a pair also.

- If your child is having great difficulty with the change in air pressure, you may need to give her a Children's Tylenol to control the pain. Your child may become fussy even after the plane lands since her ears may not have "popped" so that she is still feeling that pressure on her ears.

7. Encourage your child to drink plenty of fluids, especially water, to reduce the risk of dehydration.

8. Be respectful to the other passengers. Don't allow your child to kick the seat in front of you and don't continually flip up and down the attached tray. Also, please don't change your toddler's diaper or pull-up at your seat. Most planes have pull down change tables in the bathroom for your convenience.

9. Using a child carrier is sometimes useful after the plane has landed so that your hands are free to grab any overhead luggage. If you have a stroller waiting, you may switch her into it or just place your tote bag and carry-on items onto the stroller and head to the baggage retrieval.

How to Manage Jet Lag

If you are traveling across several time zones, you cannot escape experiencing some symptoms of jet lag which include sleepiness, reduced alertness, headaches, decreased ability to perform mental and physical tasks, night-time wakening, and a general feeling of malaise and nausea. Your jet lag becomes even more challenging when you must cope with the jet lag of your toddler.

Unfortunately, there are no simple solutions that eliminate jet lag and there is some disagreement over some of those solutions. For instance, some seasoned travelers encourage parents to give children, including toddlers, Benadryl to make them drowsy on the plane so that they sleep during the evening of the new time zone. Yet, the company that could gain from this recommendation - McNeil Consumer Healthcare, disagrees as they remind people "that right on the label of the product it says that Benadryl should not be used to make a child sleepy. In fact, others claim that by giving Benadryl to a child, you risk a hyperactive child rather than a sleeping child.

When we arrived in France, we opted to get everyone on Paris time that very day. That said, we let our daughter take some short naps to cope with the changes. We also gave her snacks on her "old" time and gave her her main meals on France time. For a couple of evenings, she went to bed an hour earlier than her home schedule so that she rose early. The first night was very difficult but within two or three days all of us were on the right time zone.

While there is no consensus on how to deal with jet lag, you may find the following list of recommendations helpful:

- Stay awake until it's bedtime. Of course, your child may be too exhausted and no matter how many distractions you give her, she may just fall asleep. Much will depend on how much sleep she had on the plane and in what time zone she was in when she had that sleep.

- If your child falls asleep when you would like to keep her awake, see if you can let her have a short nap and then waken her. Of course, you will have to brave a child who may wake crying since she is so over tired! Much will depend on how exhausted you are feeling to know how much you can tolerate.

- Let your child have a short nap when you have crossed several time zones to get acclimatized to the new time zone. Letting him have these naps can help him have a better sleep at night. You also don't want her to get so exhausted that her immune system gets compromised.

- Maintaining routines are important and during jet lag, they may be even more important. If you arrive during the day, plan on freshening up in your hotel room and then go outside. Going for a walk or playing at a playground will help you get on the new time zone and will help you have an even deeper sleep when you go to bed. Arriving at night when your body tells you it is daytime is the most difficult. You still need to get ready for bed but find some quiet activity to help you and your toddler prepare for sleep. Watch some television, read some books, listen to quiet music and then go to bed. If she wakes during the night, you may need to repeat this process before she falls asleep again.

- Try to darken the bedroom as much is possible by turning off all the lights and closing all the curtains to convince her body that it is time to sleep. That way, if your toddler wakes up during the night, the darkness will hopefully trick her mind into believing that it is night when her body believes it is daytime.

- When you plan your travel itinerary, have realistic expectations especially during the first couple of days. Find some parks to visit and enjoy being outside having leisurely walks.

- Expose your toddler to as much sunlight as you can when you first arrive since it will help her brain adjust to the new time zone.

- Some seasoned travelers recommend that if you are traveling east, try going to bed earlier a few nights before leaving, and if you are traveling west, try going to bed later for a couple of nights. If you don't think this approach will work for your toddler, you might at least consider you going to bed earlier for a few nights before your departure to ensure that you are better rested to cope with you and your child's jet lag when you reach your destination.

- Jay Olson of JetLag Rooster maintains that travelers need to figure out when to seek and avoid light based on their trip and their body clocks. Olson has created a website where you enter specifics about your trip such as the time you usually go to bed and wake up, and whether you want to adjust to jet lag a few days before departing, on the plane or after you arrive. The results offer a detailed multi-day plan that highlights the best times to avoid and seek out light. You can receive your own personalized jet lag battle plan free on this website:

http://www.jetlagrooster.com/about

CHAPTER 9:

TRAVEL BUSY BAGS

WHAT ARE BUSY BAGS?

A busy bag contains a toddler friendly activity that is stored in a resealable bag or a pencil case. The purpose of a travel busy bag is to give your child an activity that generally he can do independently or with a minimum of your involvement. Of course, your supervision is always required since your toddler might suddenly put an item in his mouth. You will find that some activities work better if you are sitting beside your toddler such as on a plane or in the back seat with her in the car. Other activities you can give your toddler when he is sitting in his stroller while you are sightseeing, while you are in a restaurant, or when you are visiting someone who has no toddlers.

CONTAINERS FOR BUSY BAGS

The following can be used as containers for busy bags. Whatever you choose, remain consistent and use the same kind of container for all your busy bags so that they will stack compactly in your On The Go bag.

- **Medium-sized Resealable Bags:** These are an economical choice. However, their disadvantage is that the plastic can tear or if it isn't properly sealed, you can lose items.

- **Binder Pencil Cases:** Our preference is zippered pencil cases that are usually stored inside a binder. Try to find pencil cases that have a transparent front so that you can easily identify what activity is in the case. I found mine at a Dollar Store. Use those binder holes to attach a group of busy bags to a binder ring.

HOW TO USE BUSY BAGS

Busy bags provide toddlers plenty of stimulation as they engage in a variety of activities. However, your child will quickly realize that you have a collection of busy bags and he may have a difficult time settling with one activity since he is aware that there may be more.

1. Set a timer on your phone and let your toddler know that she must occupy her time for ten minutes before she is given anything else. It is a way to encourage her attentiveness on the activity you provide and it is a way to stretch out your activities rather than going through them too quickly.

2. Remember your child enjoys repetition so that you can rotate a series of busy bags. When my daughter and I went on a 6 hour car ride, she used approximately 10 busy bags, interspersed with some other activities that you will be reading about such as activities with a cookie sheet.

3. **Not all busy bags will be appropriate for your child** as there is such a huge span of developmental skills between toddlers. You will need to choose busy bags that you believe are appropriate for your child

BUSY BAG ACTIVITIES

1. Include several packages of stickers with a small sticker album or a small notebook.

2. Add some finger puppets in a bag. You can buy them or make any simple finger puppets from the following websites:

   - Make simple paper puppets from: http://www.enchantedlearning.com/crafts/puppents/twofinger/

   - Make finger puppets from a child's glove: http://www.wikihow.com/Make-Finger-Puppets

   - Make felt finger puppets from: http://www.wikihow.com/Make-Felt-Finger-Puppets

3. Make some small coloring books. There is a great website, KidZone, that has Printable Itsy Bitsy Book Templates for the alphabet. Add some crayons in your bag. http://www.kidzone.ws/prek_wrksht/colors/single-books.htm

4. Place in a bag some very large pasta shells and a shoelace. Attach one piece of pasta to one end of the shoelace and tie a knot. You may need to show her how to "thread" the pasta onto the shoelace.

5. Add some stamps, stamp pad and a small notebook.

6. Add a linking toy or child's linking necklace.

7. Print some photos of friends and family and of places that you will be seeing and put them in a small 4 X 6 album book.

8. Make an Edible Bracelet. Add a licorice string and some colorful o-shaped

cereal to string onto the licorice.

9. Include a spice container that has holes large enough to insert pipe cleaners. Cut the pipe cleaners into smaller pieces and show your child how to put them in these holes.

10. Place in one of your busy bags a collection of small note cards that have some fun pictures or designs on the front. Give her practice putting them in and out of their envelopes. Add some stickers in the bag for her to decorate the inside of the cards.

11. Include some lacing cards. You can create lacing cards from the following website: http://www.activityvillage.co.uk/lacing_cards.htm.

    Print the shapes on card stock paper and laminate or use contact paper. Cut into a rectangle shape rather than cutting around the shape since it will be easier for your toddler to hold. Make holes larger than a pipe cleaner. Give your child a couple of pipe cleaners to thread through the holes.

12. Add a bag of small erasers to sort, put in patterns and stack.

13. Add a glue stick, a folded piece of construction paper, and any collage items: strips of paper, feathers, small foam shapes, and textured stickers.

14. Attach two keys to a key chain and include the two accompanying locks. She will be able to open and close the lock and decide what key is needed. Initially, you may decide to give her only one lock and key.

15. Add a box of flash cards or postcards. Encourage him to look at the pictures, stack the cards and tell you what he sees.

16. Add a couple of long bolts and matching washers and nuts to place on the bolts.

17. Add some reusable stickers into your busy bag so that she can place them on her window while traveling.

18. Add a pack of post-it notes and a small notebook. She can put the post-it notes on her window or on the pages of a small notebook.

19. Place in a bag a folded piece of black construction paper and some colored chalk. Add a small package of disposable wipes to wipe your child's hand of the chalk when he is finished.

20. Include a sheet of bubble wrap and markers in a busy bag.

21. Pack a small roll of masking tape or painter's tape with a small notebook. Add a small plastic lid so that you can cut off small strips of masking tape and attach them to the edge of the lid. She can take off these strips and add to her notebook.

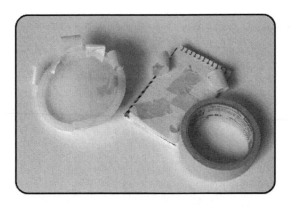

22. Fill bag with a small calculator, an old wallet filled with different business cards, and play money.

23. Include a new toy that you have gift wrapped for your child to open and play with.

24. Fold a sheet of contact paper into your busy bag to use for a collage. Include such items as small pieces of foil, tissue paper, scrapbook paper, feathers, paper clips, cotton balls or fabric pieces. When she is finished putting the items on the paper, lay the top sheet of the contact paper over the sticky side.

25. Add a small paper plate or a cardboard circle, glue and cotton balls.

26. Give her a busy bag filled with junk mail to open. Include any address labels you may also have received and a few crayons.

27. Cut out some colorful scrapbooking paper approximately 4 X 6 inches. Add

a small one hole puncher for her to cut holes in the paper. Check to make sure that the hole puncher is one that she can easily squeeze together by herself.

28. Fill a busy bag with first aid items such as Band-Aids, gauze, Q tips, cotton balls or cotton gauze. Add a glue stick and a folded sheet of construction paper.

29. Add several small wind-up toys in a busy bag.

30. Cut some colorful straws into a variety of lengths, add a folded sheet of construction paper and some scotch tape. Include a small plastic lid to attach strips of tape on the edge of the

lid. Your child can remove the tape and use it to attach the straws to the paper.

31. Include a coupon organizer. Collect various coupons and add both in your busy bag. She can organize the coupons into the various pouches. Include a crayon for her to color the coupons.

32. Add several sheets from a "Paint With Water" book. Fill an empty roll-on deodorant bottle or an Aqua-Doodle Pen with water to use to paint the sheets.

33. Place in a busy bag a small plastic vase or garden pot. Add some green painter's tape and markers. Cut the pieces of masking tape for her and she can place them on this container. Include markers and stickers for her to finish decorating the container.

34. Place some colorful craft sticks and painter's tape in the busy bag. Tell her she can create a sculpture by taping together the sticks. You will need to tear off strips of painter's tape for her to use.

35. Add a small compact mirror in a busy bag. Your toddler will enjoy opening

and shutting the case and looking in the mirror.

36. Print small coloring pages that fit into your busy bag. Laminate these sheets or use contact paper. Include some dry-erase crayons and some stickers.

37. Add any small flat wooden craft shapes. Craft stores or Dollar Store often has seasonal shapes with markers.

38. At a Dollar Store, you can find small board games that use either one or more golf tees. Add enough tees for your child to fill all the holes.

39. Include a section of a road map and two small cars.

40. Include a small puzzle or a collection of two piece puzzles in a busy bag.

41. Print some coloring pages of dinosaurs and include a sheet of sandpaper and crayons. Show her how to place the picture on top of the sandpaper before she begins to color to create a textured dinosaur. The following website, The Color, has coloring pages of dinosaurs: http://www.thecolor.com/category/coloring/dinosaur.aspx

42. Attach some ribbon to a shower hook and place in a busy bag. Let her wave them while you play uplifting music. This activity is only suitable for driving in the car not flying in a plane or eating at a restaurant!

43. Include a small notebook and on one side of the notebook, glue colorful pictures or even photos. On the left side of the notebook, take a pair of scissors and cut strips on the page. Place the cut page over the picture and as she flips the strips, she will gradually see the picture.

44. Make some popsicle stick puppets. The following website, wikiHow, gives some great ideas to make simple popsicle stick puppets: http://www.wikihow.com/Make-a-Popsicle-Stick-Puppet

45. Make a memory game and store in a busy bag. Spread the cards on a surface face down. Take turns flipping two cards over until one of you find two matching cards. If you have a young toddler, he will be happy to just flip each card over to see what it is. Memory games can be located at a Dollar Store or you can make your own. Print the following games on firm card stock paper:

- http://www.busybeekidsprintables.com/Animal-Memory-Games.html

- http://www.activityvillage.co.uk/minibeasts_matching_game.htm

46. Include some Q- tips, individual packets of cleansing wipes and a book of 'Magic Paint Posters'. These painting books can be found at a Dollar Store or Michaels. As you can see from the photo, the paints are attached to the book and you just use a wet Q tip to paint.

47. You can keep your toddler well entertained with a variety of busy bags

of playdough. Put some blue playdough in a plastic bag and include some sea creatures for an ocean theme. Give her some brown play dough for a desert theme by including some plastic desert animals. The following are more examples of what you could include:

- Dinosaurs, twigs, small rocks

- Plastic animals, plastic trees

- Several plastic cookie cutters

- Cut straws of different lengths

- Plastic sea creatures and glass gems

- Different kinds of pasta noodles

- Colorful buttons and paper clips

48. Include several playdough mats. Check out the following website to get you started:

   http://www.sparklebox.co.uk/topic/creative-arts/playdough-mats/topics.html#.Uak925WfuSK

49. Include a small paper plate and a variety of stickers.

CHAPTER 10:

COOKIE SHEET BUSY BAGS

The following busy bags need a 9 X 13 cookie sheet.

1. Choose pompoms of different colors and add magnetic strips to them. Check out the following website, Bubbles and Bobbins, to find printable pompom activities: http://www.bubblesandbobbins.com/2012/03/magnetic-pom-pom-activity.html. Place the worksheets on a cookie sheet and have your child match the pompom to the correct colored circle.

2. Include a collection of different magnets such as wild animals, sea creatures, construction vehicles, and zoo animals. The following companies make a great variety of magnets:

Smethport, Melissa & Doug, and Shure. For added fun, make some appropriate scenes to use with the magnets by choosing pages from calendars that have country scenes, city scenes, and seasons.

3. Print paper dolls such as Dora, Cinderella or a Teddy Bear and the appropriate clothing from the following website: http://www.colorcutandcreate.com/i_paper_people.php

    Cut and laminate the dolls and clothing,

and then add velcro dots to the fronts of the paper dolls and to the backs of the clothing. Another option is to use Magnetic Dress Up Dolls such as the ones made by Melissa & Doug.

4. Cut a piece of white plastic tablecloth to fit your cookie sheet. Give her dry erase crayons to draw on it. When she is finished, wet a paper towel or use a baby wipe to clean the surface.

5. Cut a sheet of flannel to fit the cookie sheet. Print any of the following templates. If possible, laminate the templates so that they will last longer. Cut out small pieces of felt or velcro and attach to the back of each template. As another option, add magnetic strips to the backs of each template and just use your cookie sheet.

- The Very Hungry Caterpillar: http://www.dltk-teach.com/books/hungrycaterpillar/felt_fun.htm

- Itsy Bitsy Spider: http://www.makinglearningfun.com/themepages/SpiderItsyBitsyFeltBoard.htm

- Five Little Monkeys Jumping On the Bed: http://www.preschoolprintables.com/felt/fivemonkeys/feltmonkey.shtml

- Flannel Pizza: Cut a tan circle for the pizza crust. Cut larger round and oval shapes of red for the tomato sauce. Cut several yellow rectangular pieces for cheese. Cut dark brown pieces in circles for the pepperoni. If she likes green pepper on her pizza, cut some small green pieces of flannel.

- There are also many packaged flannel stories you can buy such as nursery rhymes and fairy tales. You can buy them at many educational stores such as Education Station or Amazon.

6. Add a package of Wikki Stix and place it on the cookie sheet to bend and twist into different shapes. If you aren't familiar with Wikki Stix, check out their website: http://www.wikkistix.com/what_are_wikkistix.php

CHAPTER 11:

OTHER TRAVEL ACTIVITIES

FILE FOLDER GAMES

For these activities you will need to use letter size file folders.

1. On the following website, Preschool Printables, there is a file folder game for matching hearts: http://www.preschoolprintables.com/filefolder/valentine/filefolderheart.shtml.

   Print the sheets, cut out each heart and preferably, laminate them. Glue one set of hearts on the right hand side of the file folder. On the front of each glued heart, add a velcro dot. With the other set of hearts, add the accompanying side of the velcro dot. Glue an envelope on the inside of the file folder on the left hand side and place those hearts.

2. Check out the following website, Mr. Printables, to download an Ice-Cream Color Matching Game: http://www.mrprintables.com/printabl e-file-folder-games-ice-cream.html. Your child can match the colors of the ice cream scoops and the colors of the suckers with the appropriate cones and sticks.

3. Make a Shape Matching File Folder from the following website, They Call Me Granola. You can match any of the following: hearts, triangles, octagons, rectangles, triangles, squares, ovals, circles, stars, sun and moon. http://theycallmegranola.wordpress.co m/2012/08/18/file-folder-games-for-tots-preschoolers/

4. Use a cheap set of flash cards and cut them in half. On the inside of the file folder, trace the shape of the box on both sides of the folder. Glue one half of each flashcard inside that shape. Glue an envelope on the back of the file folder and add the rest of the flash card. Have your toddler match the

other half of the flashcard to the ones glued to the file folder.

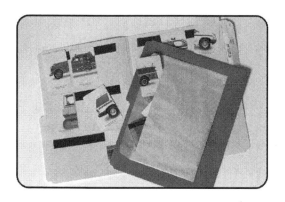

5. Make a game matching the mother animal to baby animal. Often you can find cheap flash cards so that all you need to do is glue half the cards on the inside of the file folder. Trace with a black marker the card shape beside each of the pasted cards. Consider placing two velcro dots on this surface. Add the coordinating velcro dots on the back of the cards before you place them in an envelope. Glue the envelope either on the outside or inside of the folder. If you can't find these cards, you could make your own from the following website, Kiz Club:

http://www.kizclub.com/animals.htm.
Choose Baby Animal Match.

SHEET PROTECTOR ACTIVITIES

Collect various activities from preschool
activity books, coloring books and printables
from the internet. Make sure these activities
are age appropriate, focusing mainly on
shapes and colors. Place each of these
activities in a sheet protector and attach them
together in a small binder or with just a binder
ring. Also attach to the sheets a pencil case
with dry erase crayons and a soft cloth to
clean off the sheet protectors so that the
activities can be used again. Worksheet
pictured below is from the Comprehensive
Curriculum of Basic Skills.

FINGER RHYMES

Teach your toddler some finger rhymes. The following are some suggestions:

Round and round the garden (Run forefinger round the palm)
Like a teddy bear:
One step, two step, (Jump finger up the arm)
Tickle you under there. (Tickle under the arm)

Ring the bell (Tug a lock of hair)
Knock at the door, (Tap forehead)
Peep in, (Peer into eyes)
Lift the latch, (Tweak nose),
Walk in. (Open mouth)

Two little blackbirds sitting on the hill (Start with your hands behind your back.)
One named Jack (Bring one hand to the front with your pointer finger extended.)
One named Jill (Bring your other hand to the front with pointer finger extended.)
Fly away, Jack (Put the hand and finger representing Jack behind your back.)
Fly away, Jill! (Do the same with your "Jill" hand.)

Come back, Jack! (Bring "Jack" back to front.)
Come back, Jill! (Bring "Jill" back to front.)

Dance Thumbkin dance, (Wave thumbs of both hands)
Dance Thumbkin dance
Dance ye merry men, every one: (Wag all the fingers)
But Thumbkin he can dance alone, (Wag thumbs only)
Thumbkin, he can dance alone.

Dance Foreman dance (Verse 2: Wag forefingers)
Dance Longman dance (Verse 3: Wag middle fingers)"
Dance Ringman dance, (Verse 4 Wag ring fingers)
Dance Littleman dance (Verse 5: Wag little fingers)

MUSIC

Have some children's music ready to play during your trip. Also, your child will enjoy singing some simple songs with you. The following are some suggestions for songs to sing:

- Twinkle, Twinkle Little Star
- Itsy Bitsy Spider
- Old Macdonald Had A Farm
- Row, Row Your Boat
- If You're Happy and You Know It
- Pop Goes the Weasel
- She'll Be Coming 'Round The Mountain
- I'm A Little Teapot
- Skip To My Lou
- London Bridge Is Falling Down

MUSIC RESOURCES:

Veggie Tales: 25 Favorite Travel Time Songs
Let's Go! Travel, Camp and Car Songs by Susie Tallman
Travellin' Tunes by Sharon, Lois and Bram
20 Best for Toddlers by St. John's Kids

Travel Journal

- Buy an 8" X 11" blank spiral notebook that your child can use as a travel journal. Glue some of the activities he has done while traveling. Keep an envelope of stickers at the back of this book that will be appropriate to add to this book. Have your toddler glue in tickets and pictures from brochures.

- Before you begin your trip, think about some of the things your toddler is going to see and download some appropriate coloring pages. At some of the gift shops you go into, you may also find coloring books about the area. Have him color some of the pages and then glue them in his journal.

- Add any postcards you may have bought during the day.

- Make sure you record any of his comments about what he has done each day and any fun memorable moments. When you get home, have him add some photos from his holiday.

CHAPTER 12:

SIGHTSEEING ACTIVITIES

The following are a list of suggestions to keep your child fully engaged when you are sightseeing. Many of these activities work especially well when your child is in a stroller.

Again, the developmental skills vary greatly

between 18 months and three years old. Choose the activities that will be appropriate for your child.

1. Make sure you plan at least one toddler friendly activity in your daily itinerary. Find a park or playground, zoo or swimming pool that your toddler can enjoy. It's a fun and relaxing break for everyone!

2. As you are sight seeing, have fun with your toddler by pretending you are a robot, a race car, an airplane, or a super hero. What might a robot say when it looks at a painting in the art gallery? How would a race car carry your child while wandering through a museum? Obviously, you can't be too loud since you don't want to disturb other people, but you can use your voice very expressively to keep your toddler's interest.

3. Have your child choose postcards at various sites. A toddler's language development varies a lot, but if he has enough words to express what he saw, then have him dictate to you in his own words what he saw and liked as you

write it on the back of the post card. Make sure you add any cute responses he had during the day also.

4. Declare a 'Color Day'. Each member of your family must wear something in the particular color you have chosen. Then as you go sight seeing, continually look for things in that color.

5. Declare a 'Bird Day'. Put temporary bird tattoos on everyone and then continually look for birds as you go sight seeing. Show great excitement when you see a bird. Pack a small notebook and some bird stickers. Have your child add a bird sticker on a new page each time you see a bird.

6. Have each member of the family wear a baseball cap when you go sight seeing. Have fun looking for other people who are wearing caps. At the end of the day, you might want to buy your toddler a new cap.

7. Continually look for flowers during your sight seeing. Give your child flower stickers to place in a notebook.

8. Wrap a strip of masking tape on your child's wrist with the sticky side up.

This activity works especially well if you are camping or doing some sight seeing outdoors. Have him collect small leaves, a piece of a pinecone, a flower petal, a small pebble and stick on the masking tape. If he doesn't like having this tape on his wrist, give him a small bag for collecting things.

9. Include your toddler in the conversation as you look at things. My daughter was engaged at the Louvre for hours as we pointed out various paintings. We looked for animals and specific colors. We pointed out expressions on people's faces. We talked about the clothing they wore. The conversations can be endless.

10. Make a picture chart of items that you will most likely see on your day of sight seeing. Then give your toddler a crayon to color that item when he sees it. Such items could be: dogs, cats, trees, buses, cars, trucks, sales clerk, flowers, postcards, map, etc.

11. If you are going to an art gallery, download some of the paintings and sculptures that you are going to see. Laminate the pictures and hole punch the top left hand corner. Attach with a binder clip, and carry them with you as you help your toddler find these pictures. Give him a sticker to place on each picture that he finds.

12. As you sightsee, focus on various sounds. For example, if you are walking along a city sidewalk, point out each time you hear a horn honking. Ask your toddler to tell you when he hears a horn honking. Later, begin listening for a dog barking or a bird chirping.

13. Give your child an old camera and let him take his own photos. He will not aim properly and will often only get part of a picture, but he will have fun looking at them back at the hotel.

CHAPTER 13:

WAITING IN LINES

Here are a few ideas to occupy your toddler when standing in line:

1. Standing in a long line is a good time to use your stroller. Give her a busy bag to keep her occupied.

2. If you are traveling with another adult, one adult can stand in line and let the other adult give your toddler some exercise by going for a walk.

3. If you have a Smart Phone, show her photos as this provides an enjoyable activity that can take up much of her time waiting. Also, download an appropriate app for your toddler to play on your device.

4. Play the traditional game, "I Spy" and say such things as I spy with my little

eye something that is red.

5. If you have a Smart Phone, give your child a pair of children's headphones and let him listen to some music or a story that you have recorded.

6. Practice some finger rhymes while waiting.

CHAPTER 14:

HOTEL ROOM ACTIVITIES

Tip: Many travelers recommend wiping down areas in the hotel room that have accumulated bacteria, especially the TV remote control since it is an item that toddlers like to play with. You could also wipe down light switches, the telephone, doorknobs, bedside alarm clock and the toilet flush handle. This simple and quick action may prevent your family from getting sick while you are on a holiday.

For activities in the hotel room, you can use any of the busy bags you have prepared. However, for quick and easy access with some variety, you may want to pack a bag labeled "For The Hotel" and include glue, crayons and any supplies you need for the following activities:

1. Make a collage using any travel

brochures and even the hotel room's stationary paper.

2. Have some water fun in the bathroom sink or bath tub:

- Make boats from sheets of foil and float them in the sink or bath tub

- Fill the bathtub with bubble bath. Drop the bar of hotel soap in the tub and have your toddler find it. If the hotel room is using plastic cups, he could use the cup to find the bar of soap.

- In the bathtub, see how many places your toddler can hide the soap on his body: under an arm pit, between his arm and waist, sitting on it, etc.

- Fill the sink with water and give your child his socks to wash and wring out.

3. Refer to our comments about your toddler keeping a travel journal. Have your toddler make collages, add stickers, color some pages, and you can add any cute comments or experiences that your toddler had that day.

4. Get a map from the front lobby of your hotel and give it to your toddler with several small cars. Show him how to drive his cars on the map. He could also add some stickers on the map.

5. Hide some pompoms or socks in the room for your toddler to find.

6. Give your child some folded socks to throw on top of the bed. If there is room, gradually back up and throw further away.

7. Put a folded sock on your child's head and see how far he can walk before it falls off. Have him walk on his hands and knees and carry a sock on his back.

8. Place several feathers on a table in the room. Show her how to blow the feathers off the table.

9. Have your toddler roll across the bed until you catch him on the other side.

10. Fill the sink with water and plastic sea creatures. Use the spoon that is in the hotel room to "catch" the fish.

11. Put a balled up sock on the floor. See if your toddler can pick it up with his feet.

12. Exercise together doing such activities as the following: hopping up and down, stretching arms up to the ceiling, bending down and touching your toes, moving your head sideways, moving your head up and down, patting your stomach, turning from one side to the other, standing on your toes, squatting down, placing hands on waist, etc.

13. Give your toddler socks from your family's suitcases to sort. Can she fold the matches together or even roll into balls?

14. Give your toddler a sheet of contact paper and make a collage of anything he has collected throughout the day including tickets, brochures, leaves, twigs, etc.

15. Do crayon rubs of various items your toddler has collected during the day: leaves, tickets, pine needle, etc. For instance, tape a sheet of paper over some leaves that you have collected. Show your toddler how to rub the side of the crayon over the paper covered leaves. If you haven't collected anything, give her some coins to make a crayon rub.

16. Give her a scarf, play some music and encourage her to dance as she waves the scarf around. Throw it in the air and watch it float to the ground. Play tug of war with your toddler.

17. Kneel on one side of the bed and have your toddler stand on the other side of the bed. Roll a ball back and forth across the bed.

18. Place several items on the table or bed and have your toddler identify them. Then tell him to close his eyes while you remove one of the items. Ask him what is missing. Give him clues if he doesn't know. Repeat this game until he loses interest. He may want to try removing the item for you to guess.

19. Show your toddler how to lay on the floor or on the bed and cycle with her legs. Initially, you may need to hold her ankles and help her bicycle.

20. Sit across from each other on the floor or on the bed with your feet touching. Hold each other's hands and begin to rock back and forth. Begin singing, "Row, Row, Row Your Boat".

21. Give your child some of the hotel's

stationary and let him draw on it.

22. Bring some balloons for some impromptu fun in the hotel room.

23. If your hotel has a swimming pool, take your toddler there to play.

24. Follow your night time rituals of brushing teeth, singing a song, reading a book, giving him his special blanket and holding a teddy bear etc.

We hope that we have imparted to you all the information you need to design a wonderful holiday that will be made even more special since your toddler is accompanying you. We wanted to give you information but we also wanted to increase your confidence and your enthusiasm as you plan your trip traveling with your toddler.

Bon Voyage!!

SUMMARY OF RESOURCES

BOOKS RECOMMENDED

Barton, Byron. Airport. New York: T.Y. Crowell Junior, 1982. Print.

Barton, Byron. My Car. New York: Greenwillow, 2001. Print.

Brown, Marc Tolon. Arthur's Family Vacation. Boston: Little, Brown, 1993. Print.

Cocca-Leffler, Maryann. A Vacation for Pooch. New York: Henry Holt, 2013. Print.

Cocca-Leffler, Maryann. A Vacation for Pooch. New York: Henry Holt, 2013. Print.

Cousins, Lucy. Maisy Goes on Vacation. Somerville, MA: Candlewick, 2010. Print.

Cousins, Lucy. Maisy Goes to the Museum. Cambridge, MA: Candlewick, 2008. Print.

Eastman, Peter. Fred and Ted like to Fly. New York: Beginner, 2007. Print.

Eastman, Peter. Fred and Ted's Road Trip. New York: Beginner, 2011. Print.

Hobbie, Holly. Toot & Puddle. New York: Little, Brown, 2006. Print.

Hubbell, Patricia, and Lisa Campbell Ernst. Sea, Sand, Me! New York: HarperCollins, 2001. Print.

Hubbell, Patricia, Megan Halsey, and Sean Addy. Airplanes: Soaring! Diving! Turning! New York: Marshall Cavendish, 2008. Print.

Hubbell, Patricia, Megan Halsey, and Sean Addy. Cars: Rushing! Honking! Zooming! New York: Marshall Cavendish, 2006. Print.

J., Mac Kenzie Robert. Setting Limits with Your Strong-willed Child: Eliminating Conflict by Establishing Clear, Firm, and Respectful Boundaries. Roseville, CA: Prima, 2001. Print.

Korda, Lerryn. It's Vacation Time. Somerville, MA: Candlewick, 2010. Print.

Wilkoff, William G. How to Say No to Your Toddler: Creating a Safe, Rational, and Effective Discipline Program for Your 9-month-old to 3-year-old. New York: Broadway, 2003. Print.

Williams, Sam, and Manya Stojic. Are We There Yet?

London: Boxer, 2013. Print.

PRINTABLES LINKS

"Animal Memory Games." Busy Bee Kids Printables. N.p., n.d. Web. 28 Oct. 2014. <http://www.busybeekidsprintables.com/Animal-Memory-Games.html>.

"Animals Worksheet." Kiz Club. N.p., n.d. Web. 29 Oct. 2014. <http://www.kizclub.com/animals.htm>.

"Dinosaur Online Coloring Pages | Page 1." TheColor.com. N.p., n.d. Web. 28 Oct. 2014. <http://www.thecolor.com/category/coloring/dinosaur.aspx>.

"Felt Board Pieces for Itsy Bitsy." Making Learning Fun. N.p., n.d. Web. 29 Oct. 2014. <http://www.makinglearningfun.com/themepages/SpiderItsyBitsyFeltBoard.htm>.

"Felt Board Story 5 Little Monkeys." Preschool Printables. N.p., n.d. Web. 29 Oct. 2014. <http://www.preschoolprintables.com/felt/fivemonkeys/feltmonkey.shtml>.

"File Folder / Heart Pattern Match Up." Preschool Printables. N.p., n.d. Web. 29 Oct. 2014. <http://www.preschoolprintables.com/filefolder/valentine/filefolderheart.shtml>.

"File Folder Games for Tots & Preschoolers: Color

Matching & Shape Matching." They Call Me Granola. N.p., n.d. Web. 29 Oct. 2014. <http://theycallmegranola.wordpress.com/2012/08/18/file-folder-games-for-tots-preschoolers/>.

"How to Make a Popsicle Stick Puppet." WikiHow. N.p., n.d. Web. 28 Oct. 2014. <http://www.wikihow.com/Make-a-Popsicle-Stick-Puppet>.

"How to Make Felt Finger Puppets." WikiHow. N.p., n.d. Web. 28 Oct. 2014. <http://www.wikihow.com/Make-Felt-Finger-Puppets>.

"How to Make Finger Puppets." WikiHow. N.p., n.d. Web. 28 Oct. 2014. <http://www.wikihow.com/Make-Finger-Puppets>.

"Ice Cream Color File Folder Game - Mr Printables." Mr Printables. N.p., n.d. Web. 29 Oct. 2014. <http://www.mrprintables.com/printable-file-folder-games-ice-cream.html>.

"Lacing Cards." Activity Village. N.p., n.d. Web. 28 Oct. 2014. <http://www.activityvillage.co.uk/lacing_cards.htm>

"Magnetic PomPom Activity." Bubbles+Bobbins. N.p., n.d. Web. 28 Oct. 2014. <http://www.bubblesandbobbins.com/2012/03/magnetic-pom-pom-activity.html>.

"Minibeasts Matching Game." Activity Village. N.p.,

n.d. Web. 28 Oct. 2014. <http://www.activityvillage.co.uk/minibeasts_matching_game.htm>.

"Paper Finger Puppets Craft - Enchanted Learning Software." Paper Finger Puppets Craft - Enchanted Learning Software. N.p., n.d. Web. 28 Oct. 2014.

"Preschool and Kindergarten Colors Recognition Practice Single Color Itsy Bitsy Books." Colors Recognition Practice. N.p., n.d. Web. 28 Oct. 2014.

"Print and Cut Free Paper Dolls!" Color Cut & Create. N.p., n.d. Web. 28 Oct. 2014. <http://www.colorcutandcreate.com/i_paper_people.php>.

"Topic Playdough Activity Mats for Early Years - SparkleBox." Topic Playdough Activity Mats for Early Years - SparkleBox. N.p., n.d. Web. 28 Oct. 2014. <http://www.sparklebox.co.uk/topic/creative-arts/playdough-mats/topics.html#.Uak925WfuSK>.

"The Very Hungry Caterpillar Felt Board Fun (or Puppets)." DLTK. N.p., n.d. Web. 29 Oct. 2014. <http://www.dltk-teach.com/books/hungrycaterpillar/felt_fun.htm>

REFERENCE LINKS

"Apply for a Children's Passport." U.S. Passports and International Travel. N.p., 10 Oct. 2014. Web. 29 Oct. 2014.

<http://travel.state.gov/passport/get/minors/minor s_834.html>.

"CATSA | ACTSA." Complete Items List. N.p., n.d. Web.   29   Oct.   2014. <http://www.catsa.gc.ca/complete-item-list>.

"Jet Lag Rooster." Jet Lag Rooster. N.p., n.d. Web. 29 Oct. 2014. <http://www.jetlagrooster.com/about>.

"Passports for Children." Government of Canada, Foreign Affairs and International Trade Canada, Passport Canada. N.p., n.d. Web. 29 Oct. 2014. <http://www.ppt.gc.ca/info/16-.aspx>.

"Planning Road Trips." Planning Road Trips. N.p., n.d.   Web.   29   Oct.   2014. <http://www.planningroadtrips.com/packing/car/>.

"Recommended Consent Letter for Children Travelling Abroad - Travel.gc.ca." Government of Canada. N.p., n.d. Web. 29 Oct. 2014. <http://travel.gc.ca/travelling/children/consent-letter>.

"Smart Carry-On Luggage Packing Tips." Woman's Day. N.p., n.d. Web. 29 Oct. 2014. <http://www.womansday.com/life/travel-tips/smart-carry-on-luggage-packing-tips-101797>.

"Toddler Tantrum Advice and Tricks." Parenting. N.p., n.d. Web. 29 Oct. 2014. <http://www.parenting.com/article/toddler-tantrum-advice?page=0,1>.

OTHER BUSY TODDLER, HAPPY MOM BOOKS

BUSY TODDLER, HAPPY MOM

Do you often wish you had more ideas on how to keep your child stimulated at home? Do you find yourself signing up for expensive toddler programs since they give you the confidence that you have provided all that your toddler needs for his developmental growth? Do you wish that your toddler could be more fully engaged in his play so that you have time to do the laundry? Have you purchased activity books to give you more ideas on how to entertain your toddler to discover that they are more appropriate for groups of toddlers at a daycare or for a specialized program?

If you said yes to any of these questions, this book is for you!

Busy Toddler, Happy Mom has been divided into specific chapters that work on specific skills: small motor skills, gross motor skills, arts and crafts, sensory abilities, books and language development. As these activities are introduced, you are also increasing your toddler's math and reading readiness, her vocabulary, her understanding of language, and her understanding of her world.

SENSORY PLAY

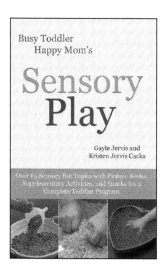

Have you given your toddler some sensory bins and discovered how much he enjoys them and you want to make more? Or have you heard about them and want to learn how to put one together? As one of our reviewers commented, "This makes it so fun being a kid!" And it makes it so much fun being a parent who can not only entertain your child but give him activities that have so many benefits:
- Encourage exploration
- Learn new concepts
- Increase creativity

- Develop small motor skills
- Expand vocabulary

You will enjoy interacting with your toddler as he learns about a variety of themes: colors, seasons, celebrations, and alphabetical topics. For further fun, we include books, a supplementary activity and an appropriate snack that will further support the topic you have chosen for your sensory bin.

This book was written as part of our Busy Toddler, Happy Mom series and therefore is suitable for your child who is over eighteen months old. However, if you also have a preschooler, this book is also really appropriate for your older child since he or she will enjoy all the sensory bins and activities but with even greater understanding of the topics.

ABOUT THE AUTHORS

Gayle Jervis has been writing curriculum ever since she taught English at a public school. She participated in starting a new course called Perspectives For Living and much of what she wrote was taken province wide to help other new teachers teach this course. When Gayle and her husband began their own family, she began writing curriculum for her own young children. When she decided to home school, her curriculum writing increased as she needed to find ways to teach two children who had two very different learning styles. During this time, she became involved in a local home school association and she became their librarian determined to build up their resources to help other home school parents. She also published a monthly newsletter for its members. Later, she became president of the association and during those two years, she hosted a large provincial home school conference. Now as her children have started their own families, she has begun once again to write appropriate curriculum especially for her two toddler grandchildren. It is her heart's desire to help moms of young toddler to harness the energy of their little people and to develop those necessary skills to prepare them for preschool.

Kristen Jervis Cacka graduated from university with a Bachelor of Commerce. Currently, she has been enjoying staying at home with her lovely daughters. As Kristen began looking for appropriate materials for her young toddler, she became frustrated by the lack of fun learning activities that could be used in a home setting. That was when she and her mom, Gayle, decided to collaborate their talents and create a series of books not only meeting her goals for her own daughter but helping other moms looking for similar activities.

37820083R00098

Made in the USA
Middletown, DE
06 December 2016